A River of Time

VOLUME 2

A River of Time

Archaeological Treasures of the Ocmulgee Corridor

DOMINIC DAY

EDITED BY S. HEATHER DUNCAN

MERCER UNIVERSITY OCMULGEE SERIES
VOLUME 2

MERCER UNIVERSITY PRESS
MACON, GEORGIA

MUP/ P654

© 2022 by Mercer University Press
Published by Mercer University Press
1501 Mercer University Drive
Macon, Georgia 31207
All rights reserved

26 25 24 23 22   5 4 3 2 1

Books published by Mercer University Press are printed on
acid-free paper that meets the requirements of the American
National Standard for Information Sciences—Permanence of
Paper for Printed Library Materials.

Printed and bound in the United States.

Text is set in Meta Pro Serif, 10.5/13;
display is set in Clarendon Text pro;
captions are set in Meta Pro, 8/9

Book design by Burt&Burt.

ISBN 978-0-88146-864-9

Cataloging-in-Publication Data is available
from the Library of Congress

Table of Contents

Photo by Sharman Ayoub.

Acknowledgments

Dedicated to the people of the Muscogee (Creek) Nation and to the people of Macon and Middle Georgia. May this work, in some small way, contribute to the rejoining of what has been separated—both the land and its creatures as well as the peoples.

Many thanks to the photographers who donated their labor and artistry to this book: Sharman Ayoub, Alan Cressler, Sylvia Flowers, Jim Gilreath, Doug Kimball, Christopher I. Smith, John Wilson, and Bobby Bond and Scott McDonald with the Georgia Department of Natural Resources.

A River of Time

VOLUME 2

The Great Temple Mound at Ocmulgee Mounds National Historical Park. *Photo by Sharman Ayoub.*

CHAPTER 1

A Crossroads of History

Every year, thousands of visitors climb the tallest of the ancient Ocmulgee Mounds in Macon, Georgia. Gazing fifty-five feet down from the top of this Great Temple Mound gives a sense of the might and mystery of the earliest Southeastern American civilization. Here, nature embraces contradiction: tall grass ripples like water next to a sprawling wetland where the water holds still, reflecting the brilliant sky.

All around rise the enormous green domes of other mounds. Among them are a funeral mound and a ceremonial earth lodge with a thousand-year-old floor in the shape of an eagle. This is Ocmulgee Mounds National Historical Park, once the greatest ceremonial center in the Southeast.

However, the park contains only the most visible of hundreds of archaeological sites along the Ocmulgee River. These vary from smaller prehistoric mounds and villages to Muscogee Indian settlements, colonial frontier forts, antebellum mills, and African American cemeteries.

For the first time, researchers have fully catalogued the rich trove of human history scattered above and below the landscape. A survey by Mercer University concludes that these cultural treasures are important to our nation because of their quantity and quality, relevance to American history, and potential for future discoveries.

The archaeological finds cover more than fifteen thousand years, the complete human record in the Southeast. But most are not in the national historical park. The Mercer study makes a strong argument that many should be.

These results come at an opportune time. The US Congress recently expanded and renamed the park, which was visited by

The Great Temple Mound rises over the wetland that lies between the mounds and the Ocmulgee River. *Photo by Sharman Ayoub.*

153,000 people in 2018. Congress also asked for a report about whether the park should be made even bigger.

There is also a sense of urgency because Ocmulgee Mounds is inside Macon. The city of 150,000 is just an hour south of ever-expanding Atlanta. The combination of international cultural significance and amazing environmental opportunities is rare among urban parks in the National Park System. Preserving history and creating an urban recreational green-space system takes time and vision, but population growth and development never pause.

A Cultural Crossroads

The waters of the Ocmulgee River have flowed from the rolling hills of the Piedmont through the coastal plain of Georgia for millions of years. On the way, they cross the fall line, which is a line of geologic change that marks the shore of an ancient sea. Large floodplains and rare ecosystems, such as chalk prairies, have formed in this transitional zone.

Cypress trees raise smooth, cramped knees beneath bald eagle nests. Black bears den in the scrubby fields that border pinewoods. As the river carved valleys and filled bottomlands, its waters supported an abundance of life.

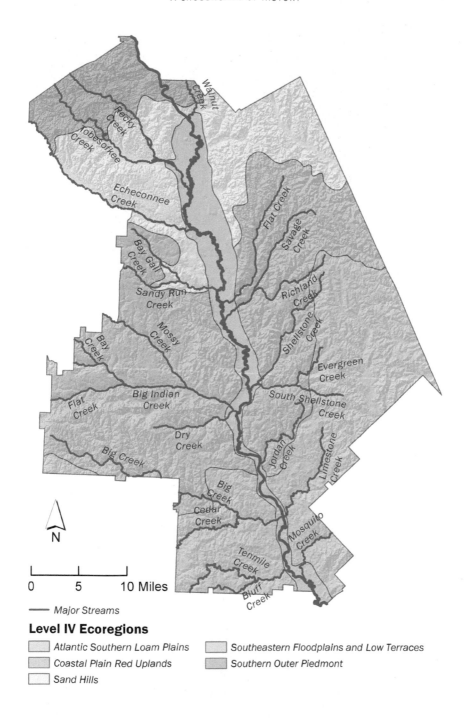

Walnut Creek

Recky Creek

Tobesofkee Creek

Echeconnee Creek

Flat Creek

Savage Creek

Bay Gall Creek

Sandy Run Creek

Richland Creek

Shellstone Creek

Mossy Creek

Evergreen Creek

Bay Creek

Flat Creek

Big Indian Creek

South Shellstone Creek

Dry Creek

Limestone Creek

Jordan Creek

Big Creek

Big Creek

Cedar Creek

Mosquito Creek

Tenmile Creek

Bluff Creek

N

0   5   10 Miles

—— Major Streams

Level IV Ecoregions

Atlantic Southern Loam Plains

Coastal Plain Red Uplands

Sand Hills

Southeastern Floodplains and Low Terraces

Southern Outer Piedmont

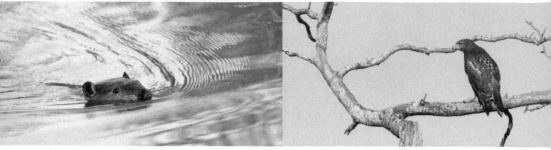

Photo by Sharman Ayoub.

A key aspect of this living diversity has been the people who have traveled the Ocmulgee and settled its rich banks over thousands of years. Nowhere is this relationship between landscape and humanity more evident than along the winding stretch of river between the cities of Macon and Hawkinsville.

This river corridor played a pivotal role in the lives of not only ancient humans, but also their Native American descendants—and, eventually, European settlers. Muscogee tribes consider the Ocmulgee Mounds and floodplain—the cradle of their civilization—to be sacred. Early frontiersmen founded a trade and banking center nearby.

Even modern efforts to chronicle this history have *made* history. During the Great Depression, archaeologists oversaw the largest-ever excavation in America. Women and African Americans played unusually prominent roles in the work.

Soon afterward, the mounds were made a national monument. Although the US Congress originally approved the park to encompass two thousand acres, only 702 acres were included until 2019. That's when Congress approved quadrupling the park's size and changing its name to Ocmulgee Mounds National Historical Park.

Congress also gave the National Park Service three years to figure out whether other land in the river corridor is important enough to be in the park, too.

The Mercer study was designed to help answer that question. The report, written by Dominic Day and Eric Klingelhofer, analyzed information about archaeological sites that had been recorded over the years in the Ocmulgee River Corridor.

Park rangers have been leading tours of the earth lodge for decades. *Courtesey NPS.*

Three generations of a family visit what was then the Ocmulgee National Monument.
Photo by Sharman Ayoub.

The 1,500-square-mile study region is anchored by the cities of Macon, Warner Robins, and Hawkinsville. The region includes Bibb, Bleckley, Houston, Pulaski, and Twiggs counties. Together, they contain almost nine hundred archaeological sites. The majority are close to each other and the river. This presents a chance to study them as a group, learning more about them in relation to each other than if the finds were isolated.

The Mercer study results support the need for growing the park along the river to Hawkinsville, perhaps by fifty thousand acres or more.

Local, state, and federal governments already own big chunks of this land. But the properties are managed piecemeal. Each has different regulations, access, staffing, and budgets.

The National Park Service study will look at whether it's both suitable and feasible to add significant cultural and natural sites in the river corridor to the National Park System. But it must also consider alternatives for preservation and interpretation by other state, local, or tribal governments.

The local Ocmulgee National Park & Preserve Initiative, formed by community members in 2011 and now a nonprofit, is building support for linking public and private lands into a single national park and preserve. This type of park would allow for public hunting and fishing to continue in places where it happens already.

But that's not the only possible outcome that the park service could recommend. It's likely to provide a menu of possible approaches from which Congress could choose.

Stone Creek winds through Bond Swamp National Wildlife Refuge.
Courtesy of U.S. Fish & Wildlife Service.

Photos by Sharman Ayoub.

Key Finds Outside the Park

For such a long-settled region, the Ocmulgee River Corridor has remained unusually untouched. When commercial river traffic ended a century ago, an economic retreat followed. That isolated the river's forests and swamps from the level of development common along Georgia's other waterways. The lack of disturbance preserved both natural ecosystems and the archaeological record.

The Ocmulgee Mounds are well known for their vast cultural significance. But lead researcher Dominick Day catalogued more than fifty *other* sites that could also be ranked among the nation's most valuable historical treasures. These vary from a former slave cemetery to a gristmill that operated for 150 years.

The most spectacular sites, however, are much older.

Mercer researchers concluded that the many rich prehistoric sites are the most significant. Fourteen of these featured ancient mounds (although some have since been disturbed). Two—besides those in the park—include more than ten mounds each. Other archaeological standouts are prehistoric villages and a cluster of sites featuring distinctive pottery.

A park that focused on a landscape of prehistoric resources would be unique in the Southeast and almost unknown in the entire National Park System.

The Opelofa Trail winds through wildflowers meadows at Ocmulgee Mounds National Historical Park. *Photo by Sharman Ayoub.*

CHAPTER 2

Evaluating Resources

Uncovering the Past, Revealing Ourselves

Archaeological resources are a foundation for our collective heritage. They provide lessons about who we are, where we have come from, and our own contemporary place within the growing chain of human experience.

But the quality of these lessons depends on the quality of the resources we preserve and study. Once archaeological resources are destroyed or lost, we lose valuable perspective on our cultural development and what it means to be a part of the human family.

Study Method and Gaps

The Mercer study started with existing records about archaeological finds. The University of Georgia maintains a database called the Georgia Archaeological Site File (GASF) to track them all (see map on follwing page).

Researcher Dominic Day sorted database entries for the five main Ocmulgee River Corridor counties. Each archaeological site record was examined and then categorized by time period, culture, type, and condition. This process provided quality control by weeding out duplicates and finding which information was wrong or missing. Spreadsheets layered information about archaeological finds with maps showing the river and its creeks as well as public land.

The study results are limited by the accuracy of the database. Some of database records aren't correct or complete—particularly those gathered before the system was computerized. Some descriptions are vague. Locations may not be exact. Several of the

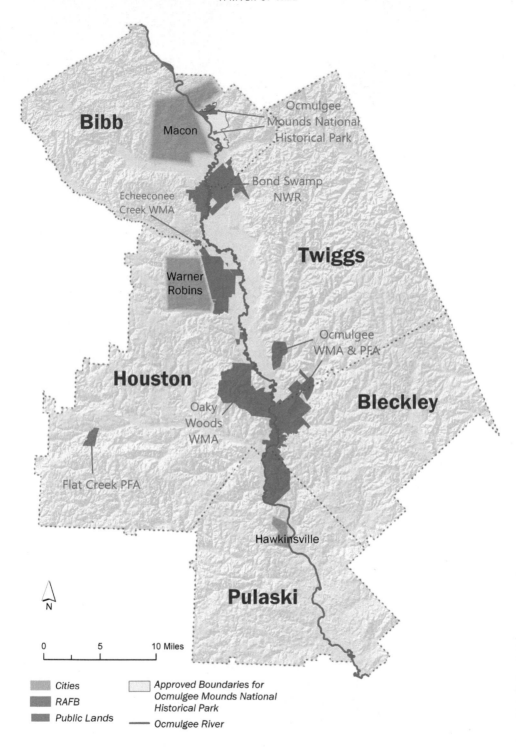

Bibb

Macon

Ocmulgee Mounds National Historical Park

Bond Swamp NWR

Echeeconee Creek WMA

Twiggs

Warner Robins

Ocmulgee WMA & PFA

Houston

Bleckley

Oaky Woods WMA

Flat Creek PFA

Hawkinsville

Pulaski

N

0   5   10 Miles

Cities
RAFB
Public Lands

Approved Boundaries for Ocmulgee Mounds National Historical Park
Ocmulgee River

sites were explored very little, so it's unclear what they contain. Other sites *were* excavated but have since been looted, so no one knows what artifacts remain.

The Most Significant Sites to American History

In addition to this sorting, researchers categorized sites from the Georgia Archaeological Site File in one more way: whether each was included in the National Register of Historic Places, or if it might belong on that list.

Why? National Register eligibility has become good shorthand for the places most important to understanding American history. This list, maintained by the National Park Service, includes buildings, sites. and districts that are significant to American architecture, archeology, engineering, history, and culture.

The places listed must also still have most of their original design, location, setting, materials, or workmanship. For example, a historic building might not make the list if it has been remodeled over and over. Those changes could remove so much historical context that the structure loses its original significance. It's no longer able to tell the same story.

Macon has thousands of buildings on the historic register, listed either individually or as part of a historic district. *Photo by Sean Pavone/iStock.*

The historic Hawkinsville courthouse. *Photo by Dominic Day.*

In the five-county study region, fifty-six sites in the database were either listed, eligible, or recommended eligible for the National Register. (The archaeologist who surveys each site notes eligibility.) Despite this, most have not received an official assessment. The number of known, important sites that haven't been evaluated shows the need for better stewardship of these cultural resources.

It's worth pointing out that cities in the study region—particularly Macon—are home to upwards of six thousand historic buildings listed in the National Register, either individually or through a historic district. However, those aren't included in this count because they are intact historic structures, rather than the archaeological sites listed in the Georgia Archaeological Site File.

To figure out how many of the archaeological sites in the Ocmulgee Corridor have broad national significance, Mercer researchers developed criteria. These melded the National Register benchmarks with those used by the National Park Service when it decides on new parks.

KEYS TO BECOMING NATIONALLY SIGNFICANT

Researchers decided that cultural sites rise to national significance if they:

- are associated with events that have made a major contribution to the broad patterns of our history;

- are associated with the lives of people important to our past;

- have special architectural value or show distinctive features of a particular time, culture, or construction method;

- collectively represent a way of life; or

- provide scientific information important to understanding human cultures occupying a landscape over time.

Applying these criteria to sites in the Ocmulgee Corridor, the study concluded that six subject areas rise to national significance:

- indigenous prehistory of the Southeast

- Muscogee origins and heritage

- Fort Hawkins and American expansion

- Great Depression and federal work program archaeology

- collective and scientific value

- resources that are not already well represented in the park system or preserved for the public

The next section highlights the Ocmulgee's most important contributions to human and American history and how they are revealed in the region's archaeological sites.

The monumental mounds at Ocmulgee were built during the early Mississippian period. The culture at this ceremonial center was unique, even compared with other mound-building societies of the time. *Photo by Sharman Ayoub.*

CHAPTER 3

Ocmulgee across Time

Traveling through time down the Ocmulgee River is a long journey: it begins with prehistoric man. The prehistoric era includes all the time before written records. In North America, this corresponds with the time before Europeans arrived.

The prehistoric era covers such a long span that historians further divide it into time periods. From earliest to latest, these are the **Paleo-Indian**, **Archaic**, **Woodland**, and **Mississippian** periods.

It should be noted that the earliest periods of human history don't always have clear boundaries. Periods are divided less by dates than by cultural change, which never happens at the same rate everywhere. The transition from one period to another, such as the Paleo-Indian to the Archaic, leaves traces in the archaeological record that are often ambiguous.

The Depression-era excavations at Ocmulgee and other ancient sites in the area unearthed thousands of artifacts. *Photo courtesy NPS.*

Ancient Origins

The first people living in the Ocmulgee area were descended from humans who traveled from East Asia into North America. This period of human occupation, from 13,500 to 8,000 B.C., is called the **Paleo-Indian** period.

In the archaeological record, Paleo-Indian sites are often identified by the presence of an early tool called the Clovis point, which resembles a large spearhead. Chips and debris from crafting stone tools are also used to recognize Paleo-Indian sites.

Ocmulgee River Corridor sites from this era are found between those of larger Paleo-Indian societies in the Savannah River Valley and along the Gulf Coast. It's possible, if not likely, that the Ocmulgee region was a crossroads even during the earliest periods of human activity in North America.

The next prehistoric time period, the **Archaic**, lasted from about 8,000 b.c. to 1,000 b.c. The earliest farming, regional trade, and monumental architecture began during this time.

Archaic people tended to settle in places with a good supply of chert, a type of sedimentary rock used for making tools. There are chert sources in Houston and Pulaski counties. Archaic artifacts also include the earliest ceramics, ground stone tools, and shaped soapstone. Soapstone was used in early vessels and slabs because it was easy to shape. The fall line became a strategic area for trading soapstone between regions.

The **Woodland** period comes next, covering 1000 b.c. to 1000 a.d. Society became more socially and politically complex

Left, clovis points like this one are a way to identify sites from the earliest human presence, during the Paleoindian period. *Photo courtesy NPS.* Right, During the Archaic period, soapstone was used in making vessels because it was easier to shape than other rock.

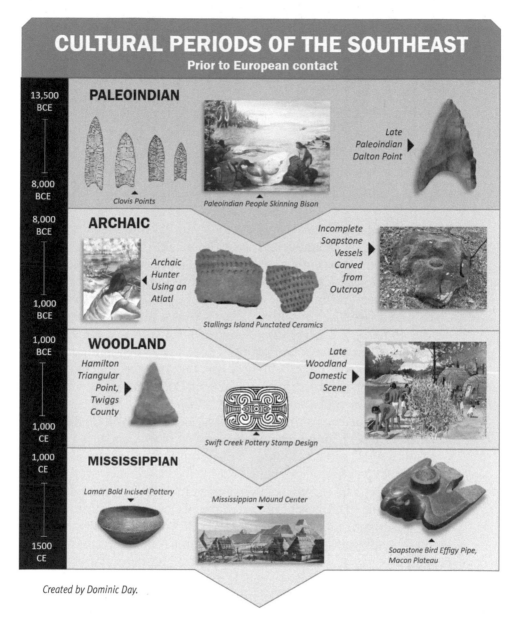

CULTURAL PERIODS OF THE SOUTHEAST
Prior to European contact

13,500 BCE – **8,000 BCE**

PALEOINDIAN

Clovis Points

Paleoindian People Skinning Bison

Late Paleoindian Dalton Point ▶

8,000 BCE – **1,000 BCE**

ARCHAIC

◀ Archaic Hunter Using an Atlatl

Stallings Island Punctated Ceramics

Incomplete Soapstone Vessels Carved from Outcrop ▶

1,000 BCE – **1,000 CE**

WOODLAND

Hamilton Triangular Point, Twiggs County ▶

Swift Creek Pottery Stamp Design

Late Woodland Domestic Scene ▶

1,000 CE – **1500 CE**

MISSISSIPPIAN

Lamar Bold Incised Pottery ▼

Mississippian Mound Center ▼

Soapstone Bird Effigy Pipe, Macon Plateau ▲

Created by Dominic Day.

during this time. Communities developed more elaborate trade networks. They began settling around farms and building flat-topped mounds.

During the middle of the Woodland period, people living along the Ocmulgee were part of a far-reaching trade web. Goods,

17

Left, this point, used in a weapon, is from the Woodland period. Center, stamped Swift Creek ceramics made along the Ocmulgee were traded as far away as the Midwest. Right, This is an example of later Swift Creek stamped pottery. *Courtesy of NPS.*

ideas, and customs traveled across a wide swath of North America, reaching as far as the Midwest and the Great Lakes.

The culture in Georgia at the time, called Swift Creek, was distinctive from other parts of this North American trade network. The **Swift Creek** culture, which gets its name from a single site on the Ocmulgee River in Bibb County, is known for elaborately decorated pottery. Abstract or geometric designs were created by pressing a carved wooden paddle into soft clay before a pot or bowl was baked. The intricately carved paddles may indicate that wood carving was common within Swift Creek culture. Swift Creek pottery was probably a valuable trade product, since it has been found as far away as Indiana, Illinois, and Ohio. Swift Creek artifacts have been found throughout the Ocmulgee Corridor.

The original Swift Creek site is a village built around a mound. Mound-building was not widespread during the Woodland period, which suggests that the village was important to the region.

The shorter **Mississippian** period that followed lasted from 1000 to 1500 a.d. Its culture arose along the Mississippi River before spreading east. Society during this time centered on corn farming and was ruled by a complex political hierarchy. Pottery from this period used grit or shell as a tempering agent, which would help bind the clay and strengthen the pottery through the baking process.

The Macon Plateau's monumental mounds were built early in the Mississippian period. While Mississippian communities shared similarities, such as religious practices, the Ocmulgee settlement was a unique expression of the culture not found elsewhere in the United States.

The spiral Lamar Mound is now overgrown with trees and shrubs, but its distinctive shape was more apparent earlier in the last century. *Courtesy of NPS.*

The community was a major political center, but it rose and fell from power in just a few centuries. Historians believe this may have been because of internal political rivalries as well as more social inequality than was typical in Mississippian culture.

Even after the decline of this "Macon Plateau" society, smaller local communities still dotted the landscape. They were part of a culture called Lamar, named after a site in Ocmulgee Mounds National Historical Park where a cluster of mounds includes an unusual mound with a spiral ramp.

The Lamar people were living in the region when the first Spanish conquistadors and missionaries arrived in the 1500s. Hernando de Soto led an expedition through what is now central Georgia in 1540. Although his exact route is disputed, he crossed the Ocmulgee River and wrote about meeting the Lamar people. (Also on the Ocmulgee, de Soto became the first to record eating barbecue in Georgia.) The arrival of Europeans marked the end of the prehistoric era in the Southeast.

Muscogee Heritage and Colonial Expansion

Native American populations declined quickly after Europeans arrived. Contact with the newcomers destabilized Indian society. It also brought disease, disrupted the food supply, and led to political infighting.

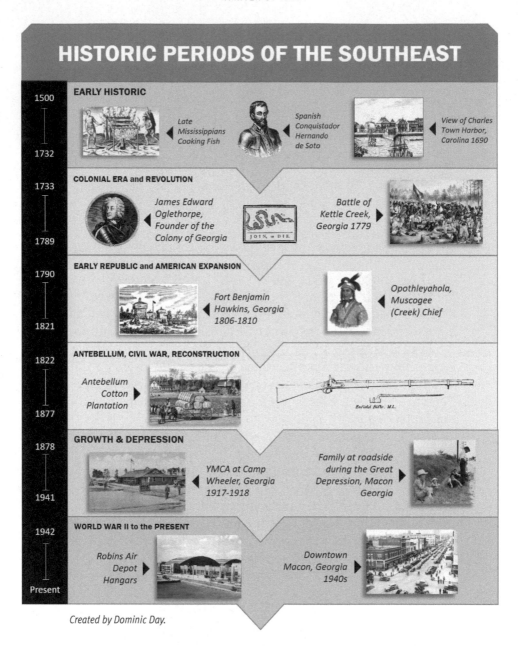

HISTORIC PERIODS OF THE SOUTHEAST

EARLY HISTORIC
1500 – 1732

Late Mississippians Cooking Fish

Spanish Conquistador Hernando de Soto

View of Charles Town Harbor, Carolina 1690

COLONIAL ERA and REVOLUTION
1733 – 1789

James Edward Oglethorpe, Founder of the Colony of Georgia

Battle of Kettle Creek, Georgia 1779

EARLY REPUBLIC and AMERICAN EXPANSION
1790 – 1821

Fort Benjamin Hawkins, Georgia 1806-1810

Opothleyahola, Muscogee (Creek) Chief

ANTEBELLUM, CIVIL WAR, RECONSTRUCTION
1822 – 1877

Antebellum Cotton Plantation

Enfield Rifle. M.I.

GROWTH & DEPRESSION
1878 – 1941

YMCA at Camp Wheeler, Georgia 1917-1918

Family at roadside during the Great Depression, Macon Georgia

WORLD WAR II to the PRESENT
1942 – Present

Robins Air Depot Hangars

Downtown Macon, Georgia 1940s

Created by Dominic Day.

It's unclear whether Lamar settlements persisted along the Ocmulgee into the seventeenth century. But many remaining Mississippian communities seem to have shifted to present-day Alabama. Eventually, Middle Georgia became home to Lamar descendants mixed with Indian populations that migrated from the Chattahoochee River Valley. They shared the *Mvskoke* language and cultural practices that began with their Mississippian ancestors, such as using yaupon holly in rituals.

The English established and operated a trading post on the Ocmulgee Plateau between 1690 and 1715. During this time, Hitchiti, Muscogee, Westos, and Yuchi Indians lived in at least eleven towns along the Ocmulgee River. The contemporary Muscogee (Creek) Nation of Oklahoma traces its political origins to this place and time.

Several decades later, the early American naturalist William Bartram recorded what he had been told about the arrival of the Muscogee at the Ocmulgee: "If we are to give credit to the account the Creeks give of themselves, this place is remarkable for being the first town or settlement, when they sat down (as they term it) or established themselves, after their emigration from the west." The common Mississippian ancestry of *Mvskoke*-speaking people tied them culturally, spiritually, and physically to the land. The Old Fields near the river and the mounds of the Macon Plateau had become part of Muscogee identity.

The Yamasee War of the 1710s, a conflict among tribes, shook up tribal alliances. Afterward, the Muscogee mostly abandoned the Ocmulgee River and retreated west to the Chattahoochee.

Soon afterward, the English colony of Georgia was founded in 1733. Its governor wanted peaceful trade relations with local tribes, who were increasingly called the "Creeks" by white settlers.

In 1805, the First Treaty of Washington officially pushed back the Creeks, making the Ocmulgee River the boundary between

At the annual Ocmulgee Indigenous Celebration, re-enactors demonstrate traditional skills and folkways that were handed down in their tribes. *Courtesy of NPS.*

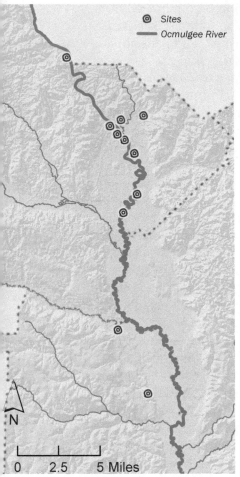

Sites
Ocmulgee River

N

0   2.5   5 Miles

This map identifies Historic Muscogee Indian sites along the Ocmulgee River corridor. *Map by Dominic Day.*

Georgia and Creek territory. The next year, a diplomatic and trading post was built near the river and the Ocmulgee Mounds. This international crossroads was named for Indian agent Benjamin Hawkins. The US Army post topped a hill that had been occupied off and on for thousands of years.

Benjamin Hawkins was able to keep peace between settlers and Native Americans in the years following the American Revolution. But after the Louisiana Purchase opened up land to settlement and the newcomers pushed west, Creeks resisted losing their territory.

The Creeks allied with the British during the War of 1812, and Fort Hawkins became a major military supply depot and garrison for soldiers fighting in the subsequent Creek War.

Fort Hawkins anchored a line of ten river forts constructed under General David Blackshear. An old Indian trail was improved to link these forts of "Blackshear's Line." Five of the forts were in the study area covered by the Mercer report. These square, wooden structures featured eight-foot-tall stockades, with two blockhouses each.

A series of removal treaties slowly pushed the Creeks out of Georgia by 1825, when they also lost ownership of the Ocmulgee Mounds. Fort Hawkins was abandoned and became a plantation. One blockhouse was moved into the city as an outbuilding.

The Civilian Conservation Corps built a replica of the Fort Hawkins blockhouse in 1938. In recent years, further excavation of the fort's palisade wall has turned up many more artifacts of the frontier era and expanded our knowledge of the fort's architecture.

After being driven from Georgia, most Muscogee people resettled in Oklahoma. But Ocmulgee remained a symbol of their identity. In fact, the Muscogee (Creek) capital in Oklahoma was named Okmulgee in honor of their tribe's birthplace.

The Muscogee are now among the largest and most diverse indigenous groups in the United States. The Muscogee (Creek) Nation has about eighty thousand enrolled citizens. Outside Oklahoma, there are independent tribal towns of Muscogee people in Alabama, Florida, Louisiana, Texas, and Oklahoma.

Many Muscogee citizens, as well as members of other tribes from across the Southeast and beyond, return to the Ocmulgee Mounds National Historical Park each year to celebrate their culture through dance, storytelling, and demonstrations. This Ocmulgee Indigenous

The block house at Fort Hawkins was reconstructed by CCC workers during the Great Depression. *Photo by Dominic Day.*

Celebration each September is the park's most popular event, with fifteen thousand visitors attending in 2018. Planning the annual festival led to more dialogue between the park and the tribes, influencing how their story is presented to the public.

Today, the National Parks Conservation Association is working with the Muscogee Creek Nation Youth Services Department

Many tribes, not just the Muscogee, send dancers and artisans to the annual Ocmulgee Indigenous Celebration at Ocmulgee National Historical Park each year. *Courtesy of NPS.*

Left, Muscogee (Creek) Chief Claude Cox and his family visited Ocmulgee National Monument in 1972. Workers excavate the funeral mound at Ocmulgee Mounds during the 1930s. *Photos courtesy NPS.*

on a program to reconnect Muscogee young people to their heritage at the park in Macon.

In 1999, the Muscogee Creek Nation successfully pushed the federal government to recognize the Ocmulgee Old Fields as the first Traditional Cultural Property (TCP) east of the Mississippi River. Traditional Culture Properties have a direct association with a living community's most deeply rooted beliefs, heritage, and customs. Not only the National Historical Park, but also parts of Bond Swamp and surrounding land are included in this TCP.

The Traditional Cultural Property does not give the tribes ownership rights. But the federal government must consult interested tribes about plans that might significantly alter the land or its cultural values.

Any activity that might disturb graves is an especially big concern. Many human remains were carried away during archaeological excavations at the Ocmulgee Mounds in the 1930s. The National Park Service has documented the removal of at least eighty bodies, some from the funeral mound, others from archaeological sites outside the current park boundary.

In 1990, the Native American Grave Protection and Repatriation Act began requiring that federal agencies give families or tribes the option of reburying the bodies of their ancestors. (It also created a process for returning thousands of artifacts, uncovered during excavation, to tribes and descendants.)

In 2017, the remains of 113 people were reburied at Ocmulgee Mounds National Historical Park. Efforts continue to return ancestors to this sacred ground, further deepening the bonds of the Muscogee people to their historical home.

A historic postcard shows a steamboat landing at Hawkinsville during the era when the Ocmulgee River was a shipping artery.

Ocmulgee and the Middle Georgia Economy

The Mercer study did not note archaeological sites in the five counties that yielded new, nationally significant information about the period between Indian removal and the Great Depression. But the role of the Ocmulgee River Corridor continued to evolve during that time, reflecting key events happening in the region.

During the early nineteenth century, trade along the Ocmulgee led to an economic boom in Macon and Hawkinsville. These cities were founded in 1823 and 1836, respectively. Steamboats, pole boats, and logging barges floated the river. Cotton plantations in the area prospered on the backs of slave laborers.

The river corridor—and Macon in particular—was a center for industry, military operations, and transportation during the late antebellum period and the Civil War. Mostly spared the war's destruction, the region surrendered to Union forces in 1865.

In the twentieth century, the Ocmulgee Corridor arose as a hub for the US military-industrial complex. During World War I, Camp Wheeler was carved out of the floodplain outside Macon to train

Left, the Warner Robins Army Air Depot was transformed into a major Air Force base during the Cold War. It remains the region's largest employer. Right, Camp Wheeler trained soldiers to fight in the U.S. Army during World War I. *Courtesy of L. Shapiro, Archives of the State of Florida.*

US Army troops. It was revived during World War II as an infantry training ground, military hospital, and prisoner-of-war camp.

Slightly further south, the Warner Robins Army Air Depot was transformed into a major air force base during the Cold War. Robins Air Force Base is critical to the region's economy as its largest single employer. A buffer zone was created to the north of the base as a crash zone for military aircraft. This has preserved some land along the river in Houston and Bibb counties, despite the rapid expansion of the surrounding Warner Robins metropolitan area. However, the base has never had a buffer on its long eastern boundary along the river, where many undocumented archaeological resources are likely to reside.

Great Depression and Federal Work Program Archaeology

Though the artifacts found in the Ocmulgee River valley are inherently valuable, the effort to understand them has found its own place in American history.

During the Great Depression, the federal government created work programs to help the millions of people left jobless and homeless. As part of this effort, a series of public works agencies paid for sweeping archaeological excavations in the Ocmulgee floodplain between 1933 and 1936. (The final funding source was the Works Progress Administration, which often gets most of the credit.)

Led by archaeologist Arthur Kelly, workers unearthed around 2.5 million artifacts, including spear points, pottery, clay figurines, bone tools, and shell jewelry. There were so many that most still haven't been fully analyzed. (More than two thousand artifacts are

Left, soaring unemployment during the Great Depression put many families, like this one in Macon, on the move. The Macon Plateau excavations helped by employing thousands. Right, chief archaeologist Arthur Kelly with his trademark pipe supervised the earth lodge excavation at Ocmulgee Mounds during the 1930s. *Courtesy of NPS.*

at the National Historical Park visitor center, but the majority are housed out of public view at the Southeast Archaeological Center in Tallahassee, Florida.)

Although excavations began with the Ocmulgee Mounds—including digging up bodies from the funeral mound—they also extended to many sites outside the current park. These included Brown's Mount, Swift Creek (with Kelly being first to recognize Swift Creek pottery as a cultural marker), Stubbs Mound, Fort Hawkins, Mossy Oak, Hawkins Point, Napier, Scott, Tuft Springs, and Cowards Landing.

The scope of the work reflected a wave of national interest in the region's history. The 1934 World's Fair in Chicago showcased a replica of the Macon Plateau mounds. Several years later, the De Soto Expedition Commission, created by the US Congress, published its analysis of the routes the early explorer traveled through the Southeast.

By 1935, the Ocmulgee archaeological project employed as many as eight hundred people, making it one of the largest of its kind in the country. Once excavations were done, the Ocmulgee National Monument was established at the end of 1936. A Civilian Conservation Corps camp was set up to develop the new park. The camp remained until 1942.

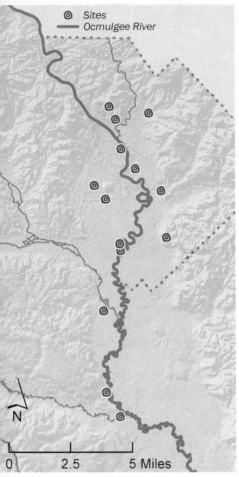

Sites
Ocmulgee River

N

0   2.5   5 Miles

Depression-Era work site locations.
Map by Dominic Day.

The WPA digs broke ground in more ways than one, reflecting changes taking place in American society.

A team of local African American women excavated the important Swift Creek site and others. This is especially noteworthy during the Jim Crow Era South. These forty women were the only known black workers employed as excavators on Ocmulgee sites. Between 1935 and 1941, only 3 percent of all WPA workers in the country were black women. Although the Depression-era job relief programs were run on federal dollars, they operated within local political systems, which were often rife with racism.

In addition to the female excavators, other women made also huge leadership contributions to the work.

Isabel Garrard Patterson, while not trained as an archaeologist, was a critical advocate for Ocmulgee archaeology and later for the creation of the Ocmulgee National Monument. As an outstanding spokeswoman for scientific archaeology in Georgia, Patterson helped get funding for the digs. She worked and communicated closely with Arthur Kelly and other prominent archaeologists in the region and often visited the excavation sites.

Decades later, one of America's earliest professional female archaeologists, Carol I. Mason, was the first to thoroughly analyze some of the artifacts uncovered at Ocmulgee. During the 1950s, she made major contributions to understanding their meaning.

These themes of gender and race that played out during the archaeological work along the river deserve further examination and interpretation for the public.

An excavation team of African American women worked at many Ocmulgee-area archaeological sites, including the Lamar Mounds (shown here). *Courtesy of NPS.*

Beyond Time

The two final criteria for national significance of the Ocmulgee Corridor focus on the value of the sites when taken together and the niche they would fill in the federal park system.

The Ocmulgee River after heavy rains as viewed from U.S. Highway 341 at Hawkinsville. *Photo by Dominic Day.*

CHAPTER 4

Ocmulgee Archaeology across the Landscape

The archaeological sites in the Ocmulgee Corridor are individually significant: like pieces of a puzzle, each highlights individual details of a big picture. But their cultural and scientific value is much greater combined as a landscape.

Having so many puzzle pieces in the Ocmulgee floodplain so close together makes them easier to connect. The result is a more seamless view of the big picture.

The landscape of artifacts could make a bigger Ocmulgee Mounds park unique, even when compared with other national parks.

For now, most of the puzzle pieces remain scattered outside the park boundary, on both public and private land near the river.

The hodgepodge of ownership and management can be confusing. To the south, private land divides the Ocmulgee Mounds from Brown's Mount and Bond Swamp National Wildlife Refuge. These are both managed by the US Fish and Wildlife Service from an office at another refuge north of the study area.

Across from the 7,800-acre Bond Swamp is Echeconnee Creek Wildlife Management Area. This WMA includes separate chunks of property scattered along the river as far north as Macon; sections further south total around 690 acres near Robins Air Force Base.

The base, plus a big stretch of privately owned land, divides Echeconnee Creek from two more wildlife management areas downstream. Ocmulgee and Oaky Woods WMAs are roughly across the river from each other. They are popular public hunting grounds, with Ocmulgee WMA also containing Ocmulgee Public Fishing Area. Together, Ocmulgee and Oaky Woods WMAs also

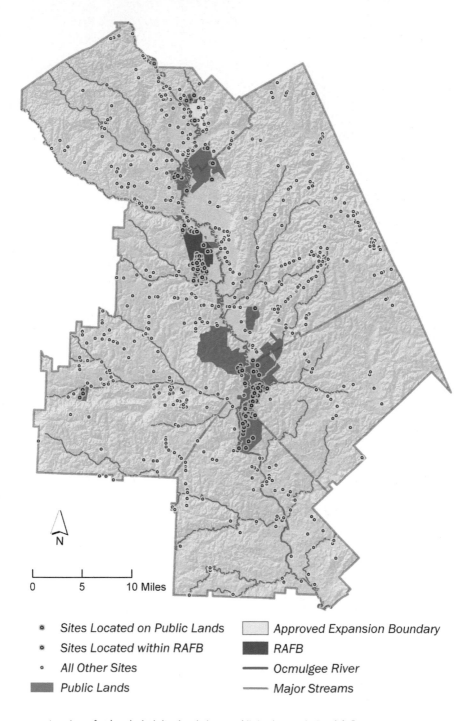

Locations of archaeological sites in relation to public lands. *Map by Dominic Day.*

Left, an angler at Ocmulgee Public Fishing Area, which is part of the study area. *Photo by Bert Deener, courtesy Georgia DNR Wildlife Resources Division.* Right, Oaky Woods Wildlife Management Area is a popular public hunting area and bear habitat along the Ocmulgee, managed by the state. *Photo by Dominic Day.*

provide the only protected parts of Middle Georgia's black bear habitat. The state of Georgia manages all the WMAs, although many are leased by the state from private owners.

Some of the most significant archaeological sites are on these public lands, although others on private land enjoy no protection at all.

A Prehistoric Prize

An expanded Ocmulgee Mounds park would be unique for the story it could tell about prehistoric life in the Southeast. Almost three-quarters of archaeological sites in the region have a prehistoric component. More than half deal with only prehistoric times.

Among all the types of archaeological finds in the river corridor, this prehistoric panorama has the greatest national significance, the Mercer study concludes.

The number, age, and undisturbed condition of the prehistoric sites is so outstanding, any park containing them would be very rare in the National Park System.

National parks always protect the archaeological resources on their properties. However, not many focus on them as their core mission. Of the 419 units that make up our national parks,

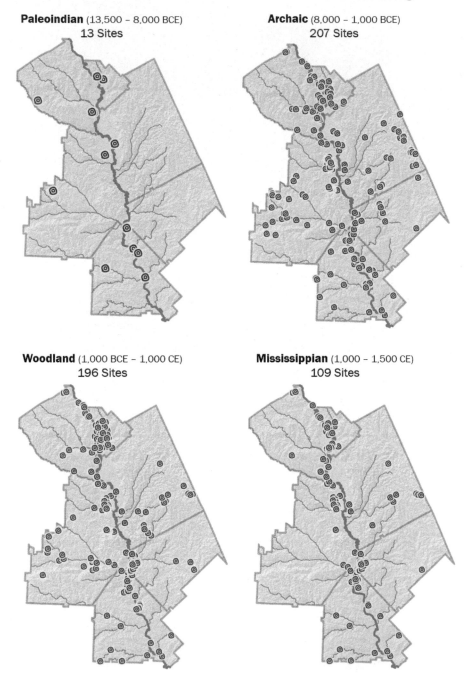

The locations of prehistoric sites, divided by time period. *Maps by Dominic Day.*

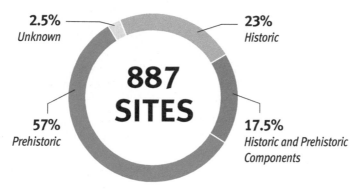

2.5%
Unknown

23%
Historic

887 SITES

57%
Prehistoric

17.5%
Historic and Prehistoric Components

Archaeological sites by major time period.

historical parks, historic sites, memorials, and monuments, Ocmulgee is one of only three that feature prehistoric resources of the Southeast. No national park properties outside the desert Southwest protect prehistoric archaeology across a landscape.

Many important archaeological sites in the Southeast are protected at the state level, but almost all of these are isolated by surrounding farms or development. (Examples are Etowah Mounds in northwest Georgia and Moundville in Alabama.)

All these factors would enable an expanded Ocmulgee Mounds park to fill a gap.

This is an important conclusion, because the park service primarily supports new parks if they protect resources that *aren't* found enough in today's park system (a characteristic the service calls "suitability"). It's part of what the current study of the Ocmulgee Corridor will evaluate.

The Ocmulgee prehistoric finds include a tremendous wealth of artifacts from every major period of human presence. The earliest sites are rarest, with only thirteen. About two hundred sites each from the slightly later Archaic and Woodland periods have been recorded. About half as many reflect Mississippian times.

Especially remarkable are those resources from the two earliest periods, artifacts of the Swift Creek culture, and the Mississippian mounds.

Artifacts at most Paleo-Indian sites in North America were either found on the surface or after the soil had been disturbed. Some of the Ocmulgee-area Paleo-Indian sites are unusually helpful because the artifacts were still encased in the layers of soil in which they were deposited. This context provides archaeologists much more information about Paleo-Indian society and its environment.

Due to the murkiness of thousands of years of time, all evidence of Paleo-Indian and Archaic culture is extremely valuable to the archaeological record—even sites that haven't been well studied and those with few artifacts. The camps and tool-making sites that dot the Ocmulgee Corridor are vital to our limited understanding of these early Americans.

Prehistoric mound sites are particularly significant because they were built in places that were long important politically, religiously, and socially. Plus, the general public already views these "Indian Mounds" as symbols of the region's ancient history.

Mercer researchers noted that there are—or were—twelve ancient mound sites *outside* the Ocmulgee Mounds National Historical Park. Yet even mounds that were heavily disturbed or razed may have valuable artifacts left, the report states.

The prehistoric sites are worth even more when studied together.

The Lamar Mounds site from the air before trees were allowed to grow on it. *Photo courtesy NPS.*

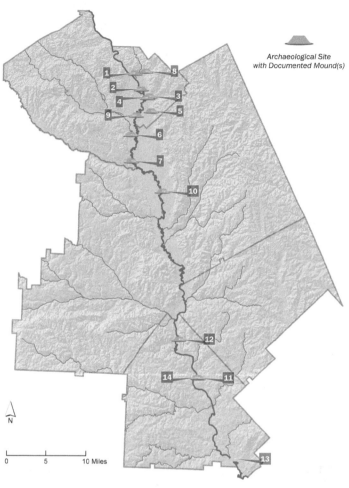

Archaeological Site
with Documented Mound(s)

N

0   5   10 Miles

NUMBER	SITE NAME	CULTURAL PERIODS	PRESERVATION STATE
1	Macon Plateau	Mississippian	Protected
2	Lamar Mounds	Mississippian, Historic Indian	Protected
3	Swift Creek	Woodland	Graded
4	Adkins	Woodland	Destroyed
5	Browns Mount	Mississippian	Unknown
6	Stubbs	Mississippian, Woodland	Unknown
7	Cowarts Landing	Mississippian, Woodland	Unknown
8	Scott	Mississippian, Woodland	Unknown
9	Adele	Mississippian	Vandalized
10	Bullards Mounds	Mississippian	Vandalized
11	Unnamed	Woodland	Razed and Redeposited
12	Shelly	Woodland	Unknown
13	Sandy Hammock	Mississippian	Razed
14	Hartford Mound	Unknown	Unknown

A Panorama of Time

Beyond the early prehistoric finds, the river corridor contains hundreds of other archaeological sites. Their *collective* significance is tremendous—especially as a source for new research. From this perspective, a landscape of cultural resources is inherently more valuable than resources in isolation. It's also extremely rare.

The most insignificant of early sites can provide new insight when examined in relation to others. As an example, the many Archaic sites, their richness in special trade goods of the time, and the presence of a rare Archaic mound show Middle Georgia was a key cultural center. Any one of the sites individually would not have allowed researchers to draw broader conclusions about the region and culture.

Preserving the Ocmulgee River Corridor would protect existing archaeological sites, most of which haven't been thoroughly investigated. Perhaps more importantly, it would also protect the many resources that currently lie undiscovered underground.

Throughout the river corridor between Macon and Hawkinsville, archaeologists have found significant artifacts anywhere they have looked. This indicates there are probably countless more sites to be found.

Some could potentially fill gaps in our knowledge about the region's history. For example, artifacts might reveal more about

Mist rises from the wetland where a boardwalk winds toward the river, as seen from the Great Temple Mound. *Photo by Sharman Ayoub.*

early river transportation or De Soto's first contacts with Native Americans. Georgia residents have begun to suggest new archaeological sites, such as the place where the steamboat *Charles Hartridge* wrecked in 1856.

Investigating these finds together would enhance our understanding of past civilization and how it shaped modern life in the Southeast. The potential for future research and enrichment of our history is tremendous.

A number of significant archaeological sites dating to ancient times are found on Ocmulgee WMA, part of which is also a Public Fishing Area. *Photo by Bert Deener, courtesy Georgia DNR Wildlife Resources Division.*

Drawn to Water

Mapping the archaeological sites shows them clustered along the Ocmulgee River and the creeks feeding it. Eighty percent are within five miles of the river or within a mile of a major tributary. Sixty-one percent are within five miles of the river itself.

A five-mile buffer was used because it captures both archaeological sites and land with a lot of conservation potential. In some places the floodplain stretches a long way from the river, as do existing public lands, such as Ocmulgee and Oaky Woods wildlife management areas. A smaller, one-mile buffer zone was used for the major streams because they flow through more developed areas.

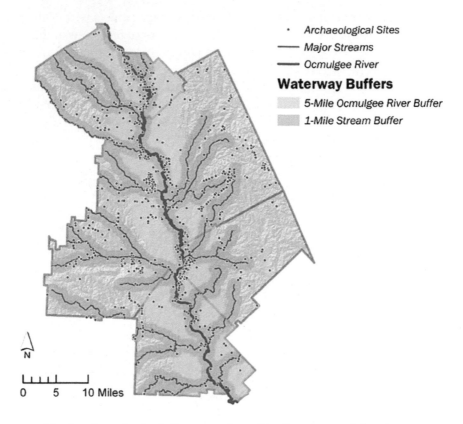

· *Archaeological Sites*
— *Major Streams*
— *Ocmulgee River*

Waterway Buffers

5-Mile Ocmulgee River Buffer

1-Mile Stream Buffer

N

0   5   10 Miles

Most archaeological sites were found in the course of clearing land for development, mining, or some other disturbance. Even so, many more have been found in the river floodplain than on the more-developed land near the creeks.

Archaeological sites are clustered along the river in Bibb County, Houston County, and at the boundary of Bleckley and Pulaski counties. All the known mound sites are close to the river.

The Mercer analysis found that Bibb, Houston, and Twiggs counties had the most archaeological sites in the study area, with more than two hundred each. Pulaski County is home to 114 sites, and Bleckley has eighty-one.

The areas where the most finds were made aren't necessarily the richest in history. Rather, they tend to be on public land like Robins Air Force Base, where surveys are required by federal law, which only applies to tribal and federal public land. State and private properties don't receive the same protection. Equally good

Archaeological sites in each study area county.

(or better) artifacts may be found near the river on property that hasn't been checked. After all, the link between archaeological sites and waterways is common. Throughout time, people often choose to travel and settle near water.

Preserving the river buffer would generally catch the most important sites. Otherwise, many will be destroyed. And most won't be studied without a coordinated research effort under single management.

The limestone outcroppings at Brown's Mount are unusual for the region. *Photo by Dominic Day.*

CHAPTER 5

Gathering Places

Exciting Finds for History and Archaeology

The Mercer report gives details about a sample of the most important archaeological sites. These were chosen from the fifty-six that are either listed on the National Register, or should be.

Mercer researchers couldn't say whether 41 percent of the sites in the study area qualify for the National Register. The state database lists the status as "unknown" if the site hasn't been investigated much. If these sites were studied, many more might turn out to be worth National Register listing.

The report also notes that archaeological sites might currently be listed for a certain type of artifact, but not all the types actually there. For example, a site might be identified as having a mound but not a burial, even if the mound contained burials.

This section provides examples of some of the most momentous finds in the Ocmulgee River Corridor, organized by time period.

Ancient Sites

Paleo-Indian sites are the earliest and rarest. An archaeological site near a Pulaski County creek has great potential for discoveries starting with this period and continuing until almost historic times, after which written records began to appear. It's been recommended for further study.

Pulaski County has some key sites from the next-earliest period, the Archaic. A site called Sandy Hammock has deep deposits of stone debris from toolmaking. Ocmulgee WMA in Pulaski is home to at least five important prehistoric sites. One is near the

A largely-unexplored but very promising ancient site is located near the Ocmulgee Public Fishing Area dam. *Photo courtesy Georgia DNR Wildlife Resources Division.*

public fishing area dam. Another has deeply deposited artifacts beneath land used as a seed farm. Both hold material such as stone and ceramic shards from the Archaic period and later.

Three other finds on Ocmulgee WMA are clustered in a way that suggests they are related. All feature pottery and stone-carving fragments from the Archaic and Woodland periods. Some have artifacts from earlier or later prehistory as well. All three sites contain Swift Creek cultural items, such as pottery, graves, or circular "pit features."

Swift Creek pottery sherd with intricate stamped pattern. *Courtesy of UGA Georgia Indian Pottery Site.*

Intricately stamped Swift Creek pottery was also found at an archaeological site near Echeconnee Creek inlet. On land leased by Robins Air Force Base, the site overlooks the floodplain in Houston County from an upland terrace. Artifacts found there show it was used from early prehistoric times until historic Creek Indians lived in the area.

Prehistoric Mounds

Most of the prehistoric mound sites are located on the border between Bibb and Twiggs counties.

As discussed earlier, the Swift Creek site is nationally important for defining an entire culture. (The archaeological site has been damaged since WPA excavations, and further research is needed to see what remains.)

Prehistoric mound sites, although uncommon generally, are plentiful near the Ocmulgee River. Across the river from the

Brown's Mount is a high point in this relatively flat region, overlooking Bond Swamp. Naturalists hike there for its profusion of lilies in April. *Photos by Dominic Day.*

national historical park is a complex of thirteen mounds with a village from the same era. This site, called Adele, is on land owned by Cherokee Brick Company. Most of the mounds are low house mounds. One has been vandalized by looters. But most of the artifacts have been preserved by layers of mud from the floodplain.

A stacked stone wall and ditch, which might have been built by a Woodland community, circles the summit of Brown's Mount. The WPA excavated the remains of an earth lodge and Mississippian mounds on the same limestone ridge. Most of the archaeological site is on land managed by the US Fish and Wildlife Service. The Ocmulgee Land Trust, with the help of the Ocmulgee National Park & Preserve Initiative, has a contract to purchase about 150 privately owned acres that include the rest of the archaeological site.

Bullards Mounds, on privately owned land in Twiggs County, is another former village with at least eleven low mounds built in the late Mississippian period. The site was excavated by Mercer University in the late 1980s and has been vandalized by looters since.

Two more mound-and-village sites in Bibb County were excavated by WPA archaeologists: Stubbs and Cowarts Landing. Both contain artifacts from the Archaic period through the Lamar culture, including some Swift Creek items.

A Bond Swamp site (left) on the Ocmulgee River near Bullards Landing. *Photos by Dominic Day.*

Stubbs is within Bond Swamp National Wildlife Refuge. Cowarts, in southern Bibb, has produced ceramics and soapstone fragments from Swift Creek and later cultures.

Historic Sites

While more than half the sites are prehistoric, 23 percent are from after European contact and 17.5 percent hold artifacts from both eras.

Many of the historic finds came from piles of debris that were essentially old garbage dumps. These are often full of construction trash such as bricks, nails, or glass. With some outstanding exceptions, the majority of the archaeological sites from the historic era aren't very significant when compared to the wealth of prehistoric sites.

Fort Hawkins remains the most important site after Europeans arrived. It is well known for its role as a trading and military post. However, the site was actually occupied for thousands of years, with artifacts from as far back as the Woodland and maybe even Archaic times. The fort, most recently excavated in 2012, is owned by the City of Macon, which has requested that the federal government grant it status as an Affiliated Area to the Ocmulgee National Historical Park.

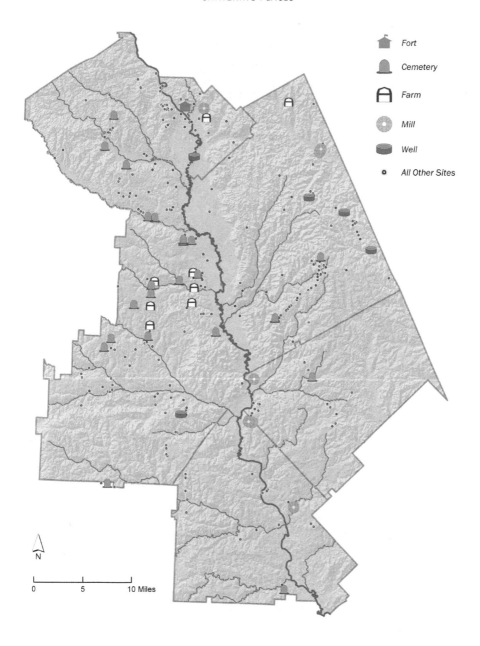

Legend:
Fort
Cemetery
Farm
Mill
Well
All Other Sites

0   5   10 Miles

N

Types of historic sites in the study area. *Map by Dominic Day.*

Some less familiar historic sites from this period are nevertheless listed on the National Register, including the remains of the town of Elberta (later changed to Warner Robins) and a nineteenth-century African American cemetery in southern Bibb County (historically called McArthur Slave Cemetery). Twiggs County is home to the site of Myrick's Mill, a gristmill that operated for at least 150 years and was visited by the Marquis de Lafayette in 1825.

Other archaeological sites from the last five hundred years include the former locations of homes, farms, cemeteries, mills, furnaces, wells, and mines.

Archaeological excavations at Fort Hawkins during the last few decades have revealed much more about frontier and military life at the fort. *Courtesy of The LAMAR Institute, Inc.*

Myrick's Mill, once visited by the Marquis de Lafayette, served Twiggs County residents for about 150 years. *Photo by Dominic Day.*

TYPES OF ARCHAEOLOGICAL SITES
IN OCMULGEE CORRIDOR COUNTIES

TYPE	COUNT	TYPE	COUNT
Airstrip	1	Isolated Artifact	6
Artifact Scatter	188	Isolated Historic	5
Brick Pile	3	Isolated Prehistoric	10
Bridge	4	Lithic Scatter	464
Burial	1	Mill	6
Camp	15	Mine	2
Cemetery	21	Mound	14
Ceramic Scatter	26	Push Pile	1
Cistern	1	Quarry	21
Dam	2	Railroad	2
Farm	8	Rock Shelter	1
Fort	1	Still	6
Furnace	3	Tavern	1
Grist Mill	1	Trash Dump	7
Habitation	7	Unknown	9
Historic Cemetery	4	Village	42
Historic Indian Scatter	1	Water Tank	1
Historic Scatter	165	Waterworks	1
Historic Village	1	Well	6
Homesite	4	Workshop	4
House/Structure	107	*Missing Data*	*23*

Stairway to the Great Temple Mound. *Photo by Sharman Ayoub.*

CHAPTER 6

In Future Park, the Past Lives

The Mercer study shows that the Ocmulgee River Corridor has been a literal crossroads of cultures for thousands of years. Sites along the Ocmulgee represent the earliest periods of human activity within the boundaries of the United States. Such a tremendous wealth of human experience has left its record within the landscape, where it is visible to those who look. At present, many are looking.

Expanding the footprint of protected land is critical. Otherwise, too many cultural treasures are at risk. Many are associated with events and themes of national significance.

Ancient American cultures are underrepresented in today's National Park System. Preserving these riches through a much larger park would fill a gap in both the nation and the region. Plus, a unified management would allow these archaeological clues to be interpreted as a landscape. This process would be illuminating to both scientists and the public.

Next Steps: Protecting Treasures, Sharing Knowledge

Congress agreeing to rename and expand the park to 2,800 acres was a huge milestone. The Ocmulgee Mounds National Historical Park Boundary Revision Act allows for the park to grow only through land donations, swaps, or purchases from *willing* sellers—and only within a specific boundary.

The act took almost five years to pass, even with the backing of local conservationists, historians, political leaders, and educators.

Bridge building. *Photo by Sharman Ayoub.*

Nonprofits such as Save Oaky Woods, the National Trust for Historic Preservation, the National Parks Conservation Association, the Georgia Conservancy, the Historic Macon Foundation, and the Ocmulgee National Park & Preserve Initiative (ONPPI) continue to build support for protecting lands within the new boundary and envisioning an even larger park connecting public lands along the river. Some, especially ONPPI, are also raising money to buy land to be included.

Those additions are underway. About three hundred acres next to the national monument were donated starting in the 1990s by the Scott and McCall families. The land wasn't accepted by the federal government, which would have had to spend more money to maintain it. But it was recognized as being worthy of the park and was held for that purpose by the Archaeological Conservancy. The nonprofit is now in the early stages of transferring the property to the park.

The ONPPI is brokering more purchases. For example, it is working through the Ocmulgee Land Trust to buy 150 acres on Brown's Mount from the estate of Steve Putnal. This would protect the entire ancient archaeological site on the ridge overlooking Bond Swamp.

Visitors to Ocmulgee National Park. *Photo by Sharman Ayoub.*

An agreement is being negotiated between ONPPI and Ocmulgee Mounds National Historical Park about how they will partner to raise money to buy more land for the park.

Many hope the new boundary is only the first step. A congressionally authorized study by the National Park Service is getting underway that could lead to Ocmulgee Mounds becoming the backbone of a much larger park.

First, the study must determine if nationally significant resources are in the river corridor outside the park between Macon and Hawkinsville. If so, the study must weigh whether creating a larger park is suitable or feasible. (Feasibility depends on several factors: potential maintenance costs as well as a size and configuration compatible with long-term protection and public use.) Ultimately, a new federal or state park could incorporate the Ocmulgee Mounds along with other public and private land. Any private land would be added only by purchasing it from willing sellers.

However, the study is also required to evaluate other possibilities for preserving any important property. Options could include management by different government agencies or nonprofits, or through partnerships. The park service must also estimate the costs of buying, operating, and maintaining any larger version of the park—whether it's a larger historical park, a national park and preserve, national recreation area, a collaboration, or some other alternative.

The process must include opportunities for public comment and feedback. The park service will also consult with Indian tribes, interested nonprofits, and agencies (such as the Georgia Department of Natural Resources and the US Fish and Wildlife Service) that already manage some of the most pristine land along the Ocmulgee.

No later than March 2022, the secretary of the Interior must deliver the study results to the House Committee on Natural Resources and Senate Committee on Energy and Natural Resources.

It's likely that this report will include a slate of alternatives for how large the park could be, what it would be called, and who should manage it. But the Interior secretary is also required to make some specific recommendations.

Some of these alternatives would boost the local economy, according to a 2017 report by University of Tennessee economists, commissioned by the National Parks Conservation Association. A national park and preserve could lead to a six-fold increase in visitation within fifteen years and add $206.7 million in annual economic activity, the study found.

People who want to celebrate, preserve, and enjoy Middle Georgia's history and environment will be invited to take part in this process. The result could be a park unlike any other in the Southeast.

It also represents an opportunity to continue the tradition of the Ocmulgee River as a vital center of cultural interaction—from the original Mississippian temple worshipers to modern-day visitors from across the globe.

The ancestors of the Muscogee left an extensive legacy as the oldest known society in the Southeast. Evidence of their contribution is embedded in the land itself. The Ocmulgee River Corridor presents a rare opportunity to preserve a landscape of archaeological resources that will deepen our shared American identity—its past, present, and future.